## The starting point: from *Inside the Black Box*

In 1998 we published this booklet's predecessor *Inside the Black Box* (Black & Wiliam, 1998b). Over 20,000 copies have been sold and the work is widely quoted. Since then we have learnt a great deal about the practical steps needed to meet the purpose expressed in the booklet's sub-title: *Raising standards through classroom assessment.*

The first part of *Inside the Black Box* set out to answer three questions. For the first of these:

*Is there evidence that improving formative assessment raises standards?*

the answer was an unequivocal yes, a conclusion based on a review, by Black & Wiliam (1998a), of evidence published in over 250 articles by researchers from several countries. There have been few initiatives in education with such a strong body of evidence to support a claim to raise standards. This positive answer led naturally to the second question:

*Is there evidence that there is room for improvement?*

Here again, the published evidence gave a clear and positive answer, presenting a detailed picture which identified three main problems. The first was that the assessment methods that teachers use are not effective in promoting good learning. The second was that marking and grading practices tend to emphasise competition rather than personal improvement. The third problem was that assessment feedback often has a negative impact, particularly on pupils with low attainments who are led to believe that they lack 'ability' and are not able to learn.

However, for the third question the answer was less clear:

*Is there evidence of how to improve formative assessment?*

Whilst the evidence provided many ideas for improvement, it lacked the detail that would enable teachers to implement them in classroom practice. It was argued that what teachers needed was: *A variety of living examples of implementation, by teachers with whom they can identify and from whom they can both derive conviction and confidence that they can do better, and concrete examples of what doing better means in practice.* Since that booklet was published, we have planned and implemented a programme in which a group of teachers has been supported in developing innovative practices in their classrooms, drawing on the ideas in the booklet. Whilst this has amply confirmed the original proposals, it has also added a wealth of new findings which are both practical and authentic. Thus, we are now confident that we can set out sound advice for the improvement of classroom assessment.

In the sections that follow, we first describe this work, and the evidence that it did raise standards. We then set out the main findings, starting with those relevant to classroom work, and then discuss the more fundamental issues involved. A final section sets out recommendations for taking these ideas forward in schools.

## The journey: learning with teachers

In this section, we recount briefly our new findings which form the basis for subsequent sections.

### The KMOFAP project

To carry out the exploratory work that was called for, we needed to collaborate with a group of teachers willing to take on the risks and extra work involved, and to secure support from their schools and their LEAs. The funding for the project was provided through the generosity of the Nuffield Foundation. We were fortunate to find, in the Medway and Oxfordshire LEAs, advisory staff who understood the issues and who were willing to work with us. Each authority selected three secondary schools, spanning a range of catchment backgrounds; they included one boys' and one girls' school, the other four being mixed. Each school selected two science and two mathematics teachers. We discussed the plans with the head of each school, and then called the first meeting of the 24 teachers – so in January 1999 the King's-Medway-Oxfordshire Formative Assessment Project (KMOFAP) was born.

The ways in which the partners involved worked together will be written up elsewhere. For the present purpose, it is the outcomes that are important. The findings presented here are based on the observations of classrooms by the King's team, records of meetings of the whole group, interviews with and writing by the teachers, and a few discussions with pupil groups. Whilst we worked initially in science and mathematics, the work has been extended more recently to involve teachers of English in the same schools.

### Spreading the word

Throughout the development of the project, members of the King's team have responded to numerous invitations

to talk to other groups of teachers and advisers; over three years they have made over 100 such contributions. These have ranged across all subjects, and across both primary and secondary phases. In addition, there has been sustained work with some primary schools. All of this makes us confident that our general findings will be of value to all, although some important details may vary between different age groups and different subjects.

A USA version of *Inside the Black Box* has been published (Black & Wiliam 1998b) and a group at Stanford University obtained funding from their National Science Foundation to set up a similar development project, in collaboration with King's, in Californian schools. We acknowledge that extension of our work has been made possible by this funding.

## National policies

The KMOFAP project has been guided by a steering group that included, in addition to the King's and LEA staff, nominees from DfES, QCA and TTA. The project benefited from this guidance and the contacts in the group have also helped us to ensure that its progress was well known to the organisations represented. The Assessment Reform Group (ARG), who initially set in train the work that led to

*Inside the Black Box* also has links with these national bodies; it has published a booklet, *Beyond the Black Box* (ARG, 1999), which gives useful guidance about policies for implementing formative assessment. These links have ensured that *Assessment for learning* is one of the central themes of the Government's Key Stage 3 initiative. Late in 2001 discussions about the project's findings took place with groups from OFSTED, DfES and QCA. Researchers and teachers in the project have been appointed as consultants to the new national programme in Scotland to develop assessment for learning.

## The learning gains

From our review of the international research literature, we were convinced that enhanced formative assessment would produce gains in pupil achievement, even when measured in such narrow terms as national curriculum tests and examinations. At the outset we were clear that it was important to have some indication of the kinds of gains that could be achieved in real classrooms, and over an extended period of time. Since each teacher in the project was free to decide the class with which they would work on these ideas, we discussed what data were available within the school, and set up a 'mini-experiment' for each teacher.

Each decided what was to be the 'output' measure for their class. For year 11 classes this was generally the GCSE grades achieved, and for year 9 classes it was generally the score or level achieved in the national curriculum tests. For other classes, a variety of measures were used, including end-of-module-test scores and marks on the school's end-of-year examinations.

For each project class, the teacher identified a control class. In some cases this was a parallel class taught by the same teacher in previous years (and in one case in the same year). In other cases, we used a parallel class taught by a different teacher and, failing that, a non-parallel class taught by the same or a different teacher. Where the project and the control classes were not strictly parallel, we controlled for possible differences in ability by the use of 'input' measures, such as scores on the NFER's Cognitive Abilities Test, or school test scores from the previous year.

This meant that the size of the improvement was measured differently for each teacher. For example, a year 11 project class might outperform the control class by half a GCSE grade, but another teacher's year 8 project class might outscore its control class by 7% on an end-of-year exam. To enable us to aggregate the results across the teachers,

we adopted a common 'measuring stick' called the standardised effect size. This was calculated by taking the difference between the scores of the experimental and control groups, and then dividing this by the standard deviation, which is a measure of the spread in the scores of the groups.

For the 19 teachers for whom we had reliable data, the average effect size was around 0.3. This is equivalent to just under half a level at key stage 2, just over half a level at key stage 3, and just over half a grade at GCSE. Such improvements, produced across a school, would raise a school in the lower quartile of the national performance tables to well above average. It is clear, therefore, that, far from having to choose between teaching well and getting good national curriculum test and examination results, teachers can actually improve their pupils' results by working with the ideas we present here.

It is relatively easy for any teacher or school to make a similar analysis of their own data. Full advice on how to do this may be found on the King's College London website.

## The findings: how change can happen

This section, which forms the core of this booklet, sets out our main findings about classroom work under four headings: questioning, feedback through marking, peer- and self-assessment, and the formative use of summative tests. Most of the quotations are taken from pieces written by the teachers: the names of the teachers and of the schools are pseudonyms, as our policy was to guarantee their anonymity.

### Questioning

Many teachers do not plan and conduct classroom dialogue in ways that might help pupils to learn. Research has shown that many leave less than one second after asking a question before, if no answer is forthcoming, asking another question, or answering their own question (Rowe, 1974). A consequence of such short 'wait time' is that the only questions that 'work' are those that can be answered quickly without thought, i.e. questions that call for memorised facts. In consequence, the dialogue is at a superficial level. As one teacher put it:

*I'd become dissatisfied with the closed Q & A style that my unthinking teaching had fallen into, and I would frequently be lazy in my acceptance of right answers and*

*sometimes even tacit complicity with a class to make sure none of us had to work too hard…They and I knew that if the Q & A wasn't going smoothly, I'd change the question, answer it myself or only seek answers from the 'brighter students'. There must have been times (still are?) where an outside observer would see my lessons as a small discussion group surrounded by many sleepy onlookers.*
James, Two Bishops School

The key to changing such a situation is to allow longer wait time. Many teachers find it hard to do this – they have to break their established habits and, as they change, the expectations of their pupils are challenged:

*Increasing waiting time after asking questions proved difficult to start with – due to my habitual desire to 'add' something almost immediately after asking the original question. The pause after asking the question was sometimes 'painful'. It felt unnatural to have such a seemingly 'dead' period, but I persevered. Given more thinking time students seemed to realise that a more thoughtful answer was required. Now, after many months of changing my style of questioning I have noticed that most students will give an answer and an explanation (where necessary) without additional prompting.*
Derek, Century Island School

One teacher summarised the overall effects of her efforts to improve the use of question and answer dialogue in the classroom as follows:

*Questioning*
- *My whole teaching style has become more interactive. Instead of showing how to find solutions, a question is asked and pupils given time to explore answers together. My year 8 target class is now well-used to this way of working. I find myself using this method more and more with other groups.*

*No hands*
- *Unless specifically asked, pupils know not to put their hands up if they know the answer to a question. All pupils are expected to be able to answer at any time, even if it is an 'I don't know'.*

*Supportive climate*
- *Pupils are comfortable with giving a wrong answer. They know that these can be as useful as correct ones. They are happy for other pupils to help explore their wrong answers further.*

*Nancy, Riverside School*

Increasing the wait time can lead to more pupils being involved in question and answer discussions, and to an increase in the length of their replies. One particular way to increase participation is to ask pupils to brainstorm ideas, perhaps in pairs, for two to three minutes prior to the teacher asking for contributions. Overall, a consequence of such changes has been that teachers learnt more about the pre-knowledge of their pupils, and about any gaps and misconceptions in that knowledge, so that their next moves could address the learners' real needs. To exploit such changes it is necessary to move away from the routine of limited factual questions and to refocus attention on the quality and the different functions of classroom questions. An example is the use of a 'big question': an open question, or a problem-solving task, which can set the scene for a lesson by evoking a broad-ranging discussion, or by prompting small group discussions, so involving many pupils. However, if this is to be productive, both the responses that the task might evoke and the ways of following up these responses have to be anticipated. Collaboration between teachers to exchange ideas and experiences about questions is very valuable. The questions themselves then become a more significant part of teaching, with attention focused on how they can be used to explore and then develop pupils' learning.

*I chose a year 8 middle band group and really started to think about the type of questions I was asking – were they just instant one-word answers, what were they testing – knowledge or understanding, was*

*I giving the class enough time to answer the question, was I quickly accepting the correct answer, was I asking the girl to explain her answer, how was I dealing with the wrong answer? When I really stopped to think I realised that I could make a very large difference to the girls' learning by using all their answers to govern the pace and content of the lesson.*

*Gwen, Waterford School*

Effective questioning is also an important aspect of the impromptu interventions that teachers make once the pupils are engaged in an activity. These often include simple questions such as 'Why do you think that?' or 'How might you express that?', or – in the 'devil's advocate' style – 'You could argue that...'. This type of questioning can become part of the interactive dynamic of the classroom and can provide an invaluable opportunity to extend pupils' thinking through immediate feedback on their work.

Overall, the main suggestions for action that have emerged from the teachers' experience are:

- More effort has to be spent in framing questions that are worth asking, i.e. questions which explore issues that are critical to the development of pupils' understanding.

- Wait time has to be increased to several seconds in order to give pupils time to think and everyone should be expected to have an answer and to contribute to the discussion. Then all answers, right or wrong, can be used to develop understanding. The aim is thoughtful improvement rather than getting it right first time.

- Follow-up activities have to be rich, in that they provide opportunities to ensure that meaningful interventions that extend the pupils' understanding can take place.

Put simply, the only point of asking questions is to raise issues about which the teacher needs information or about which the pupils need to think.

Where such changes have been made, experience has shown that pupils become more active as participants, and come to realise that learning may depend less on their capacity to spot the right answer and more on their readiness to express and discuss their own understanding. The teachers also shift in their role, from presenters of content to leaders of an exploration and development of ideas in which all pupils are involved.

## Feedback through marking

It is the nature, rather than the amount, that is critical when giving pupils feedback on both oral and written work. Research experiments have established that, whilst pupils' learning can be advanced by feedback through comments, the giving of marks – or grades – has a negative effect in that pupils ignore comments when marks are also given (Butler, 1988). These results often surprise teachers, but those who have abandoned the giving of marks find that their experience confirms the findings: pupils do engage more productively in improving their work.

Many teachers will be concerned about the effect of returning pupils' work with comments but no marks. There may be conflicts with school policy:

*My marking has developed from comments with targets and grades, which is the school policy, to comments and targets only. Pupils do work on targets and corrections more productively if no grades are given. Clare [King's researcher] observed on several occasions how little time pupils spend reading my comments if there were grades given as well. My routine is now, in my target class, to:*

*i) not give grades only comments*

*ii) give comments that highlight what has been done well and what needs further work*

*iii) give the minimum follow-up work expected to be completed next time I mark the books.*

*Nancy, Riverside School*

Initial fears about how pupils might react turned out to be unjustified, and neither parents nor OFSTED inspectors have reacted adversely. Indeed, the provision of comments to pupils helps parents to focus on the learning issues rather than on trying to interpret a mark or grade. We now believe that the effort that many teachers devote to marking homework may be misdirected. A numerical mark does not tell pupils how to improve their work, so an opportunity to enhance their learning has been lost.

A policy of improving their comments requires more work initially, as teachers have to attend to the quality of the comments that they write on pupils' work. Collaboration between teachers to share examples of effective comments can be very helpful, and experience will lead to more efficient fluency. There is, however, more involved because comments only become useful feedback if pupils use them to guide further work, so new procedures are needed:

*After the first INSET I was keen to try out a different way of marking books to give pupils a more constructive feedback. I was keen to try and have a more easy method of monitoring pupils' response to my comments without having to trawl through their books each time to find out if they'd addressed my comments. I implemented a comment sheet at the back of my year 8 class's books. It is A4 in size and the left-hand side is for my comments and the right-hand side is for the pupils to demonstrate by a reference to the page in their books where I can find the evidence to say whether they have done the work…The comments have become more meaningful as the time has gone on and the books still only take me one hour to mark.*

*Sian, Cornbury Estate School*

We have met a variety of ways of accommodating the new emphasis on comments. Some teachers cease to assign marks at all, some enter marks in record books but do not write them in the pupils' books, whilst others give marks only after a pupil has responded to their comments. Some teachers spend more time on certain pieces of work to ensure that they give good feedback and, to make time for this, either do not mark some pieces, or mark only a third of their pupils' books each week, or involve the pupils in checking straightforward tasks.

A particularly valuable method is to devote some lesson time to rewriting selected pieces of work, so that emphasis can be put on feedback for improvement within a supportive environment. This can change pupils' expectations about the purposes of classwork and homework.

As they tried to create useful comments, many of the teachers realised that they needed to reassess the work that they had asked pupils to undertake. They found that some tasks were useful in revealing pupils' understandings and misunderstandings, but that others focused mainly on conveying information. So some activities were eliminated, others modified, and new and better tasks actively sought.

Overall, the main ideas for improvement can be summarised as follows:

- Written tasks, alongside oral questioning, should encourage pupils to develop and show understanding of the key features of what they have learnt.

- Comments should identify what has been done well and what still needs improvement, and should give guidance on how to make that improvement.

- Opportunities for pupils to follow up comments should be planned as part of the overall learning process.

The central point here is that, to be effective, feedback should cause thinking to take place.

Implementation of such reforms can change the attitudes of both teachers and pupils to written work: the assessment of pupils' work will be seen less as a competitive and summative judgement and more as a distinctive step in the process of learning.

## Peer-assessment and self-assessment

Pupils can only achieve a learning goal if they understand that goal and can assess what they need to do to reach it. So self-assessment is essential to learning (Sadler, 1989). Many who have tried to develop self-assessment skills have found that the first and most difficult task is to get pupils to think of their work in terms of a set of goals. Insofar as they do, so they begin to develop an overview of that work so that it becomes possible for them to manage and control it for themselves: in other words, they are developing the capacity to work at a meta-cognitive level.

In practice, peer-assessment turns out to be an important complement to self-assessment. Peer-assessment is uniquely valuable because pupils may accept, from one another, criticisms of their work, which they would not take seriously if made by their teacher. Peer work is also valuable because the interchange will be in a language that pupils themselves would naturally use, and because pupils learn by taking the roles of teachers and examiners of others (Sadler, 1998):

*As well as assessing and marking (through discussion and clear guidance) their own work they also assess and mark the work of others. This they do in a very mature and sensible way and this has proved to be a very worthwhile experiment. The students know that homework will be checked by themselves or another girl in the class at the start of the next lesson. This has lead to a well-established routine and only on extremely rare occasions have students failed to complete the work set. They take pride in clear and well-presented work that one of their peers may be asked to mark. Any disagreement about the answer is thoroughly and openly discussed until agreement is reached.*

*Alice, Waterford School*

The last sentence of this quotation brings out an important point – when pupils do not understand an explanation, they are likely to interrupt a fellow pupil when they would not interrupt a teacher. In addition to this advantage, peer-assessment is also valuable in placing the work in the hands of the pupils. The teacher can be free to observe and reflect on what is happening and to frame helpful interventions:

*We regularly do peer marking – I find this very helpful indeed. A lot of misconceptions come to the fore and we then discuss these as we are going over the homework. I then go over the peer marking and talk to pupils individually as I go round the room.*
                                    *Rose, Brownfields School*

However, self-assessment will only happen if teachers help pupils, particularly the low-attainers, to develop the skill. This takes time and practice:

*The kids are not skilled in what I am trying to get them to do. I think the process is more effective long term. If you invest time in it, it will pay off big dividends, this process of getting the students to be more independent in the way that they learn and taking the responsibility themselves.*
                                    *Tom, Riverside School*

One simple and effective idea is for pupils to use 'traffic light' icons, labelling their work green, amber or red according to whether they think they have good, partial or little understanding. These labels serve as a simple means of communication of pupils' self-assessments. Pupils may then be asked to justify their judgements in a peer group, so linking peer- and self-assessment. This linkage can help in the development of the skills and the detachment needed for effective self-assessment.

Another approach is to ask pupils first to 'traffic-light' a piece of work, and then to indicate by hands-up whether they put green, amber or red; the teacher can then pair up the greens and ambers to deal with problems between them, whilst the red pupils can be helped as a group to deal with their deeper problems. For such peer-group work to succeed, many pupils will need guidance about how to behave in groups, e.g. in listening to one another and taking turns.

In some subjects, making pupils familiar with grade or level descriptions is also very helpful. Pupils can be given simplified versions of examination board criteria, or encouraged to rewrite them or to create their own. Again peer- and self-assessment are intimately linked. Observations made in several English classrooms saw children engaged in peer assessment apply lessons learned during this activity to their own work. A frequently heard comment was 'I didn't do that either' or 'I need to do that too'.

Pupils' reflection about their understanding can also be used to inform future teaching – their feedback can indicate where more time needs to be spent on some topics and where it can be saved on others. A useful guide is to ask pupils to 'traffic-light' an end-of-topic test in the first lesson on the topic: the amber and red items can be used to re-adjust priorities within the teaching plan. Our experience of work on this theme leads to the following recommendations for improving classroom practice:

- The criteria for evaluating any learning achievements must be made transparent to pupils to enable them to have a clear overview both of the aims of their work and of what it means to complete it successfully. Such criteria may well be abstract – concrete examples should be used in modelling exercises to develop understanding.

- Pupils should be taught the habits and skills of collaboration in peer-assessment, both because these are of intrinsic value and because peer-assessment can help develop the objectivity required for effective self-assessment.

- Pupils should be encouraged to keep in mind the aims of their work and to assess their own progress to meet these aims as they proceed. They will then be able to guide their own work, and so become independent learners.

The main point here is that peer- and self-assessment make unique contributions to the development of pupils' learning – they secure aims that cannot be achieved in any other way.

## The formative use of summative tests

The practices of self- and peer-assessment can be applied to help pupils prepare for examinations, for example in tackling the following problem:

> *They did not mention any of the reviewing strategies we had discussed in class. When questioned more closely it was clear that many spent their time using very passive revision techniques. They would read over their work doing very little in the way of active revision or reviewing of their work. They were not transferring the active learning strategies we were using in class to work they did at home.*
>
> *Tom, Riverside School*

To change this situation, pupils can be asked to 'traffic-light' a list of key words or topics on which the test will be set. The point of this is to stimulate the pupils to reflect on where they feel their learning is secure, which they mark in green, and where they need to concentrate their efforts, in amber and red. These traffic lights then form the basis of a revision plan. Pupils can be asked to identify questions on past examination papers that test their red areas and then work with books and in peer groups to ensure that they can successfully answer those questions.

The aftermath of tests can also be an occasion for formative work. Peer marking of test papers can be helpful, as with normal written work, and is particularly useful if pupils are required first to formulate a mark scheme, an exercise which focuses attention on criteria of quality relevant to their productions. After peer marking, teachers can reserve their time for discussion of the questions that give particular difficulty; peer tutoring can tackle those problems encountered by only a minority.

A further idea has been introduced by research studies (Foos et al., 1994; King, 1992) which have shown that pupils trained to prepare for examinations by generating and then answering their own questions out-performed comparable groups who prepared in conventional ways. Preparation of test questions calls for, and so develops, an overview of the topic:

*Pupils have had to think about what makes a good question for a test and in doing so need to have a clear understanding of the subject material. As a development of this, the best questions have been used for class tests. In this way the pupils can see that their work is valued and I can make an assessment of the progress made in these areas. When going over the test good use can be made of groupwork and discussions between pupils concentrating on specific areas of concern.*
*Angela, Cornbury Estate School*

These developments challenge common expectations. Some have argued that formative and summative assessments are so different in their purpose that they have to be kept apart, and such arguments are strengthened by experience of the harmful influence that narrow 'high-stakes' summative tests can have on teaching. However, it is unrealistic to expect teachers and pupils to practise such separation, so the challenge is to achieve a more positive relationship between the two. This section has set out ways in which this can be done: they can all be used for tests where teachers have control over the setting and the marking, but their application may be more limited for tests where the teacher has little or no control.

Overall, the main possibilities for improving classroom practice are as follows:

- Pupils should be engaged in a reflective review of the work they have done to enable them to plan their revision effectively.

- Pupils should be encouraged to set questions and mark answers to help them, both to understand the assessment process and to focus further efforts for improvement.

- Pupils should be encouraged through peer- and self-assessment to apply criteria to help them understand how their work might be improved.

The main overall message is that summative tests should be, and should be seen to be, a positive part of the learning process. By active involvement in the test process, pupils can see that they can be beneficiaries, rather than victims, of testing because tests can help them improve their learning.

## Reflections: some underlying issues

In this section we reflect on the deeper issues about learning and teaching that have been provoked, not least amongst the teachers involved, by the changes that are entailed by improved assessment for learning.

### *Learning theory*

One of the most surprising things that happened during the early inset sessions was that the participating teachers asked us to run a session on the psychology of learning. In retrospect, perhaps, we should not have been so surprised. We had, after all, stressed that feedback functioned formatively only if the information fed back to the learner was used by the learner in improving performance. But whilst one can work out after the event whether or not any feedback has had the desired effect, what the teachers needed was to be able to give their pupils feedback that they knew in advance was going to be useful. To do that they needed to build up models of how pupils learn.

So the teachers came to take greater care in selecting tasks, questions and other prompts to ensure that the responses made by pupils actually helped the teaching process. Such responses can 'put on the table' the ideas that pupils bring to a learning task. The key to effective learning is to then find ways to help pupils restructure their knowledge to build in new and more powerful ideas. In the KMOFAP classrooms, as the teachers came to listen more attentively to the pupils' responses, they began to appreciate more fully that learning was not a process of passive reception of knowledge, but one in which the learners were active in creating their own understandings. Put simply, it became clear that, no matter what the pressure to achieve good test and examination scores, learning cannot be done for the pupil; it has to be done by the pupil.

Pupils came to understand what counted as good work through exemplification. Sometimes this was done through focused whole-class discussion around a particular example; at others it was achieved through pupils using criteria to assess the work of their peers.

Engaging in peer- and self-assessment is much more than just checking for errors or weaknesses. It involves making explicit what is normally implicit, and thus requires the pupils to be active in their learning. As one pupil wrote:

*After a pupil marking my investigation, I can now acknowledge my mistakes easier. I hope that it is not just me who learnt from the investigation but the pupil who marked it did also. Next time I will have to make my explanations clearer, as they said 'It is hard to understand' ... I will now explain my equation again so it is clear.*

The pupils also became much more aware of when they were learning, and when they were not. One class, which was subsequently taught by a teacher not emphasising assessment for learning, surprised that teacher by complaining: 'Look, we've told you we don't understand this. Why are you going on to the next topic?' While pupils in tune with their learning can create difficulties for teachers, we believe that these are problems we should want to have.

## Subject differences

From hearing about research, and from discussing ideas with other colleagues, the teachers built up a repertoire of generic skills. They planned their questions, allowed appropriate wait time, and gave feedback that was designed to cause thinking. They ensured that pupils were given time in lessons to evaluate their own work, and that of others.

However, after a while it became clear that these generic strategies could go only so far. Choosing a good question requires a detailed knowledge of the subject, but this is not the knowledge that is gained from advanced study in a subject. A high level of subject qualification is less important than a thorough understanding of the fundamental principles of the subject, an understanding of the kinds of difficulties that pupils might have, and the creativity to think up questions that can stimulate productive thinking. Furthermore, such pedagogical content knowledge is essential in interpreting responses – what pupils say will contain clues to aspects of their thinking that may require attention, but picking up on these clues requires a thorough knowledge of common difficulties in learning the subject. Thus, although the general principles of formative assessment apply across all subjects, the ways in which they manifest themselves in different subjects may differ. We have encountered such differences in making comparisons between teachers of mathematics, science and English.

In mathematics, pupils have to learn to use valid procedures and to understand the concepts that underpin these. Difficulties can arise when they learn strategies that only apply in limited contexts but do not realise that these are inadequate elsewhere. Questioning must then be designed to bring out these strategies for discussion and to explore problems in the understanding of the concepts so that the need to change can be grasped. In such learning, there is usually a well-defined correct outcome. In more open exercises, as in investigations of the application of mathematical thinking to everyday problems, there may be a variety of good solutions; then an understanding of the criteria of quality is harder to achieve and may require an iteration in discussion between examples and the abstract criteria which they exemplify.

In science, the situation is very similar. There are many features of the natural world for which science provides a 'correct' model or explanation. However, outside school, many pupils acquire different ideas. Examples are the belief that, whilst animals are living, trees and flowers are not because they don't move, or the belief that astronauts seem almost weightless on the moon because there is no air there. Many of these 'alternative conceptions' can be anticipated for they have been well documented. What has also been documented is that mere presentation of the 'correct' view has been shown to be ineffective. The task in such cases is to open up discussion of such ideas, and then provide feedback that challenges them by introducing new pieces of evidence and argument that support the scientific model.

There are other aspects for which an acceptable outcome is less well-defined. As in mathematics, open-ended investigations call for different approaches to formative assessment. Even more open are issues about social or ethical implications of scientific achievements, for there is no 'answer', and so the work has to be 'open' in a more fundamental way. Then the priority in giving feedback is to challenge pupils to tease out their assumptions and to help them to be critical about the quality of any arguments.

In English, peer- and self- assessment have a long history. It follows from the nature of the subject and the open outcome of many of the tasks characteristically set, that they are central to one of its overall aims – which is to enhance the critical judgement of the pupils.

A second important function of peer- and self-assessment was brought out by Sadler (1989), who argued that criteria alone are unhelpful in judging the quality of a piece of work or in guiding progression because there will always be too many variables. The key lies in knowing how to interpret the criteria in any particular case – which involves 'guild knowledge'. Teachers acquire this through assessing pupils' work and it is this process that allows them to differentiate between grades and gain a sense of how progression is achieved. Peer- and self-assessment provide similar opportunities for pupils to be apprenticed into the guild, provided the criteria of quality are clearly understood.

In English, as with science and mathematics, attention needs to be given to the central activities. Those that are the most successful are those rich tasks that provide pupils with an opportunity either to extend their understanding of a concept within the text or to 'scaffold' their ideas before writing. Characteristically, these include small group and pair work, the reflections often being fed back into a whole class discussion. Again, this type of work is not uncommon in English, the skill being to make the task sufficiently structured to scaffold learning but not so tightly defined as to limit thinking. Such activities not only provide pupils with a chance to develop their understanding through talk, they also provide the teacher with the opportunity to give feedback during the course of a lesson through further questioning and guidance. The better the quality of the task the better the quality of the interventions.

Differences between learning tasks can be understood in terms of a spectrum. At one end are 'closed' tasks with a single well-defined outcome, at the other are 'open' tasks with a wide range of acceptable outcomes. Tasks in English are mainly at the open end, e.g. the writing of a poem, but there are closed components, eg for grammatical or genre conventions. Tasks in (say) mathematics are more often closed, but applications of mathematics to everyday problems can require open-ended evaluations. Thus, in varying measure, the guidance needed for these two types of learning work will be needed in all subjects.

Despite these differences, experience has shown that the generic skills that have been developed do apply across subjects. One of the project's science teachers gave a talk to the whole staff about his experiences, and subsequently found that other teachers:

> *do more of it than us as part of their normal teaching. Art and drama teachers do it all the time, so do technology teachers (something to do with open-ended activities, long project times, and perhaps a less cramped curriculum?). But an English teacher came up to me today and said: 'Yesterday afternoon was fantastic. I tried it today with my year 8s, and it works. No hands up, and giving them time to think. I had fantastic responses from kids who have barely spoken in class all year. They all wanted to say something and the quality of answers was brilliant. This is the first time for ages that I've learnt something new that's going to make a real difference to my teaching'.*
>
> *James, Two Bishops School*

## Motivation and self-esteem

Learning is not just a cognitive exercise: it involves the whole person. The need to motivate pupils is evident, but it is often assumed that this is best done by offering such extrinsic rewards as merits, grades, gold stars and prizes. There is ample evidence that challenges this assumption.

Pupils will only invest effort in a task if they believe that they can achieve something. If a learning exercise is seen as a competition, then everyone is aware that there will be losers as well as winners: those who have a track record as losers will see little point in trying. Thus, the problem is to motivate everyone, even though some are bound to achieve less than others. In tackling this problem, the type of feedback given is very important. Many research studies support this assertion. Examples are:

- Pupils told that feedback '...will help you to learn' learn more than those told that 'how you do tells us how smart you are and what grades you'll get'; the difference is greatest for low attainers (Newman & Schwager, 1995).

- Those given feedback as marks are likely to see it as a way of comparing themselves with others (ego-involvement), those given only comments see it as helping them to improve (task-involvement): the latter group out-performs the former (Butler, 1987).

- In a competitive system, low attainers attribute their performance to lack of 'ability', high attainers to their effort; in a task-oriented system, all attribute to effort, and learning is improved, particularly amongst low attainers (Craven et al. 1991).

- A comprehensive review of research studies of feedback showed that feedback improved performance in 60% of them. In the cases where it was not helpful, the feedback turned out to be merely a judgement or grading with no indication of how to improve (Kluger & DeNisi, 1996).

In general, feedback given as rewards or grades enhances ego – rather than task – involvement. It can focus pupils' attention on their 'ability' rather than on the importance of effort, damaging the self-esteem of low attainers and leading to problems of 'learned helplessness' (Dweck 1986). Feedback that focuses on what needs to be done can encourage all to believe that they can improve. Such feedback can enhance learning, both directly through the effort that can ensue, and indirectly by supporting the motivation to invest such effort.

# The big idea: focus on learning

Our experiences in the project all point to the need to rethink a teacher's core aim – enhancing pupils' learning. To achieve this calls for a willingness to rethink the planning of lessons, together with a readiness to change the parts both teacher and pupils play in supporting the learning process.

## A *learning environment: principles and plans*

Improvement in classroom learning requires careful forethought:

> *Actually thinking about teaching has meant that I have been able to come up with ideas and strategies to cope with whatever has arisen, and has contributed greatly to my professional development. I now think more about the content of the lesson. The influence has shifted from 'What am I going to teach and what are the pupils going to do?' towards 'How am I going to teach this and what are the pupils going to learn?'*
>
> *Susan, Waterford School*

One purpose of a teacher's forethought is to plan to improve teaching actions. So, for example, the planning of questions and activities has to be in terms of their learning function:

*I certainly did not spend sufficient time developing questions prior to commencing my formative training...Not until you analyse your own questioning do you realise how poor it can be. I found myself using questions to fill time and asking questions which required little thought from the students. When talking to students, particularly those who are experiencing difficulties, it is important to ask questions which get them thinking about the topic and will allow them to make the next step in the learning process.*

*Derek, Century Island*

Of equal importance is care for the quality of the responses that teachers make, whether in dialogue or in marking homework. Effective feedback should make more explicit to pupils what is involved in a high-quality piece of work and what steps they need to take to improve. At the same time it can enhance pupils' skills and strategies for effective learning.

There is also a deeper issue here. A learning environment has to be 'engineered' to involve pupils more actively in the tasks. The emphasis has to be on the pupils doing the thinking and making that thinking public. As one teacher said:

*There was a definite transition at some point, from focusing on what I was putting*

*into the process, to what the students were contributing. It became obvious that one way to make a significant sustainable change was to get the students doing more of the thinking. I then began to search for ways to make the learning process more transparent to the students. Indeed, I now spend my time looking for ways to get students to take responsibility for their learning and at the same time making the learning more collaborative.*

*Tom, Riverside School*

Collaboration between teachers and pupils and between pupils themselves can produce a supportive environment in which pupils can explore their ideas, hear alternative ideas in the language of their peers, and evaluate them:

*One technique has been to put the students into small groups and give each student a small part of the unit to explain to their colleagues. They are given a few minutes' preparation time, a few hints, and use of their exercise books. Then each student explains their chosen subject to the rest of their group. Students are quick to point out such things as, 'I thought that the examples you chose were very good as they were not ones in our books. I don't think I would have thought of those.' Or, 'I expected you to mention particles more when you were explaining the difference between liquids and gases.' These sessions have proven invaluable, not only to me, in being able to*

*discover the level of understanding of some*
*students, but to the students too.*

*Philip, Century Island*

An additional advantage of such an environment is that a teacher can work intensively with one group, challenging their ideas and assumptions, knowing that the rest of the class are working hard.

So the main actions to be taken to engineer an effective learning environment are:

- Plan classroom activities to give pupils the opportunity to express their thinking so that feedback can help develop it.

- Formulate feedback so that it guides improvement in learning.

- Use activities that demand collaboration so that everyone is included and challenged, and train pupils to listen to and respect one another's ideas.

- Be sure that pupils are active participants in the lessons. Emphasise that learning may depend less on their capacity to spot the right answer and more on their readiness to express and discuss their own understanding.

## A *learning environment: roles and expectations*

It is one thing to plan new types of classroom activity; quite another to put them into practice in ways that are faithful to the aims that they were developed to serve. Here there are no recipes for all to follow in a uniform way. *Inside the Black Box* was clear in stating that the effective development of formative assessment would 'only come about if each teacher finds his or her own ways of incorporating the lessons and ideas that are set out above into her or his own patterns of classroom work'.

A second principle is that the learning environment envisaged requires a classroom culture that may well be unfamiliar and disconcerting for both teachers and pupils. The effect of the innovations implemented by our teachers was to change the 'classroom contract' between the teacher and the pupil – the rules, usually implicit, that govern the behaviours that are expected and seen as legitimate by teachers and pupils.

For the pupils, they have to change from behaving as passive recipients of the knowledge offered by the teacher to becoming active learners who could take responsibility for, and manage, their own learning.

For the teachers, courage is necessary. One of the striking features of the project was the way in which, in the early stages, many spoke about the new approach as 'scary', because they felt that they were going to lose control of their classes. Towards the end of the project, they described this same process not as a loss of control, but one of sharing responsibility for the class's learning with the class – exactly the same process, but viewed from two very different perspectives. In one perspective, the teachers and pupils are in a delivery-recipient relationship, in the other they are partners in pursuit of a shared goal:

*What formative assessment has done for me is made me focus less on myself but more on the children. I have had the confidence to empower the students to take it forward.*

*Robert, Two Bishops School*

What has been happening here is that everybody's expectations, i.e. what teachers and pupils think that being a teacher or being a pupil requires you to do, have been altered. Whilst it can seem daunting to undertake such changes, they do not have to happen suddenly. Changes with the KMOFAP teachers came slowly and steadily, as experience developed and confidence grew in the use of the various strategies for enriching feedback and interaction. For example,

many started by using questions to encourage thinking, then improved their oral and written feedback so that it took thinking forward, and went on to develop peer- and self-assessment.

To summarise, expectations and classroom culture can be changed by:

- Changing the 'classroom contract' so that all expect that teacher and pupils work together for the same end, the improvement of everyone's learning.

- Empowering pupils to become active learners, taking responsibility for their own learning.

- Incorporating the changes in the teacher's role one step at a time, as they seem appropriate.

- Sustained attention to, and reflection on, assessment for learning issues.

# What next – what you can do

## *As an individual teacher*

To incorporate some of the ideas about formative assessment into your practice, the first step is to reflect on what you do at the moment. Discussion with colleagues, and observation of each other's lessons, can help such reflection. A next step must be to try out changes.

Wholesale change can be too risky and demanding – so in any case it is best to think of one thing you feel confident to try, be it traffic lights, peer-assessment, improved questioning, whatever, and try it, at secondary with just one group, at primary with just one curriculum area. We found that, as teachers explored the power of allowing pupils, in just one area or group, to tell them what they know and what they need to know, and as they gained confidence in doing this, they decided that they must extend assessment for learning to the whole of their teaching.

Progress can then be made by taking on further strategies. Where several colleagues are collaborating, they can each start with different strategies, and then share findings. This should lead to explicit formulation of an 'action plan'. A plan would comprise a set of strategies to be used, in combination, preferably starting with a class at the beginning of the school year so that there can be time to accustom both teacher and pupils to a new way of working. The experience of a year's sustained work, with only a few classes, preferably alongside similar innovations by colleagues, can provide a firm basis for subsequent adoption of new practices on a wider scale.

## Working with colleagues

Collaboration with a group that is trying out similar innovations is almost essential. Mutual observation and the sharing of ideas and experiences about the progress of action plans can give help and support both with the specific techniques and at a strategic level. Support for colleagues is particularly important in overcoming those initial uncertainties when engaging in the risky business of changing the culture and expectations in the classroom.

## Across the whole school

For any innovations, support from school management is essential. One way to support is to help teacher peer-groups find time to meet on a regular basis so that they can work together effectively. Opportunities should also be found for them to report to faculty and staff meetings.

The work of any group experimenting with innovations is an investment for the whole school, so that support should not be treated as indulgence for idiosyncratic practices. Indeed, such work should be integrated into a school improvement plan, so that evaluation of findings, and dissemination of fruitful practices, should be anticipated as a future development that should follow, and be based on, evaluation of a group's experiences.

At the same time, there may be a need to review current school policies. Policies can actually, or by interpretation, constrain use of formative assessment. A notable example would be a policy that, by demanding that a mark or grade be given on every piece of homework, prevents the serious use of comments. Five of the schools in the KMOFAP project have, following the experience of their science and mathematics teachers, modified their policies to allow comment-only marking; for two of these the modification was that no marks or grades be given on homework throughout the school. Another example would be that a target-setting system that requires very frequent review will inhibit any change in learning methods, which might slow down immediate 'progress' in order to produce medium- to long-term gains in learning skills. Those engaged in innovations may need formal exemption from such policies.

It follows that support, evaluation and subsequent dissemination of innovation in assessment for learning will only be planned in a coherent way if responsibility for strategic oversight of the development is assigned to a member of the school leadership team.

Our experience supports the view that to realise the promise of formative assessment by leaving a few keen individuals to get on with it would be unfair to them, whilst to do it by a policy requiring all staff immediately to change their personal roles and styles in their classrooms would be absurd. What is needed is a plan, extending over at least three years, in which a few small groups are supported for a two-year exploration, and they then form a basis of experience and expertise for disseminating within the school and supporting their colleagues in making similar explorations for themselves.

## Further resources

Only a few references to the literature are given here. Further information about publications and other resources can be obtained on the King's College London website in the research pages of the King's Department of Education & Professional Studies. Some of the publications can be downloaded from this site. The address is: http://www.kcl.ac.uk/depsta/education

These pages include references to other useful websites.